MW01069375

Animal Life Series

WHITE SOX

The Story of the Reindeer in Alaska

By William T. Lopp

Superintendent of Education
of Natives of Alaska
Formerly Chief of Alaska Division
United States Bureau of Education
and Superintendent of Reindeer
in Alaska

Illustrated with drawings by

H. Boylston Dummer

1927
Yonkers-on-Hudson, New York
WORLD BOOK COMPANY
2126 Prairie Avenue, Chicago

WORLD BOOK COMPANY

THE HOUSE OF APPLIED KNOWLEDGE

Established 1905 by Caspar W. Hodgson
YONKERS-ON-HUDSON, NEW YORK
2126 PRAIRIE AVENUE, CHICAGO

To the minds of most children and a good
many older persons, reindeer suggest Santa
Claus, and no more. But the reindeer is
one of man's very necessary domestic animals; it affords a means for reclaiming vast
sub-Arctic regions that now lie waste; and
in Alaska the government of the United
States has introduced reindeer and encour-
aged the raising of them, till now they are
a source of wealth to the territory. To tell
the story of the reindeer in our northerly
territory is the purpose of the present little
volume. Mr. William T. Lopp, the author,
has been concerned with the government's
work in giving the reindeer to the natives
of Alaska since the work was begun in the
'90's, and it was he who drove a herd of
reindeer seven hundred miles for the relief
of the whalers at Point Barrow in 1897.
This story of *White Sox* is, then, the work
of an authority on the reindeer; and the
publishers feel that it is worthy of its place in
Animal Life Series beside *Matka*, Dr. David
Starr Jordan's classic story of the fur seal

ALS: LWS-2

PRINTED IN U. S. A.

Printing Statement:

Due to the very old age and scarcity of this book,
many of the pages may be hard to read due to the
blurring of the original text, possible missing pages,
missing text and other issues beyond our control.

Because this is such an important and rare work, we
believe it is best to reproduce this book regardless of
its original condition.

Thank you for your understanding.

WHITE SOX

"In they plunged, together, in too great a hurry to notice
the resinous substance." (*See page* 24.)

CONTENTS

ACKNOWLEDGMENT

The author is under great obligations to his friend Mrs. Isabel Ambler Gilman, formerly a teacher in the Alaska schools and well known as the author of *Alaska: The American Northland* and *Alaskaland*, for her criticism and revision of this book in manuscript form. He wishes to express here his sincere appreciation of the valuable assistance which she rendered.

INTRODUCTION

Tнıs story will be read by boys and girls in Alaska who know their fathers' herds of reindeer "like a book," or better than a book; and it will be read by other boys and girls who never saw a reindeer and think of them only as strange and wonderful creatures that live among the snows in a far-off northern region. I hardly know whether we enjoy more hearing the story of our own domestic animals or the story of strange animals that we have never seen. So I can hardly guess whether this story will be read with more interest in Alaska or in Maine and Florida and California. But it will be read with lively interest wherever it may go.

When I was Commissioner of Education at Washington, in the Department of the Interior, people often asked me how it happened that my office had anything to do with such a distant and unrelated activity as the reindeer industry. I told them that this was one of the finest examples of real education for real life with which I had ever had to do. I found the subject tremendously interesting. Dr. Sheldon Jackson, who introduced domestic reindeer into Alaska, was then alive and was one of the most vigorous and adventurous and interesting members of my staff. Very soon Mr. Lopp, who was at that time a District Superintendent in Alaska, came on to Washington to arrange with the new Commissioner for the more complete organi-

zation of the reindeer industry and for its further
development.

I found Mr. Lopp one of those rare men who
think more than they talk. We very soon got
together, became acquainted with each other, and
settled down to the work that we had to do together. I learned to appreciate his intimate knowl-
edge of the reindeer business and its use in the
making of better living conditions and a better life
for those Alaskans who live in the reindeer country.
I learned to value his personal devotion to the great
work in which he was engaged. The friendship
that grew up between us, through our official rela-
tions, is one which I have greatly prized, from that
time down to the present day; and accordingly I
have welcomed this story of his most warmly, and
I am sure it will be welcomed by a wide circle of
readers.

ELMER ELLSWORTH BROWN

New York University

WHITE SOX

"Not a thing could he see except his mother."

I

ASTRAY FROM THE HERD

WHITE SOX opened his eyes, winked them several times, and looked about him. Not a thing could he see except his mother. She was resting on a bed of moss close beside him, wide awake, chewing her cud. He knew he had not slept very long because it was still daylight. But the daylight was gray and damp, for the sides and roof of his bedroom were of fog, — fog so thick that it walled them in completely.

"Mother," he said anxiously, "do you think we shall ever find our way back to the big herd?"

Mother Reindeer looked at him for a moment

without speaking, and went on grinding the wad
of food in her mouth — chew, chew, chew. Then
she turned her head this way and that, as if listening for any sound that might be heard.

"I'm beginning to think the whole world is made
of fog," complained White Sox. "We've been
wandering about in it for two days — here and
there, up and down — without so much as scent-
ing another reindeer or hearing a sound. Mother,
I'm getting dreadfully worried."

Mother Reindeer looked at him again. Her
kind eyes were full of patience. She did not seem
a bit worried about things like fog or being lost.

White Sox thought they had gone straying in
search of better moss fields and had become separated from the herd by the heavy mist. He never
dreamed that his mother was taking him to school.
No, indeed!

"Mother," he said, speaking a little louder,
"what if we have been going farther away all the
time and never find our way back to the big herd
on the sea beach?"

Mother Reindeer swallowed her cud. "Non-
sense!" she answered. "When the fog lifts we
shall be able to see where we are. We have better
moss here than down on the sea beach, and no
mosquitoes to bother us. There's nothing to worry
about."

"But, mother! it is very lonesome here. There
isn't a fox or a ptarmigan, not even an owl or a
mouse," White Sox complained.

Then he rose and stretched himself. He was five months old, and he had never been away from the sea beach before. He tried to look through the fog — this way and that way — but he was afraid of losing sight of his mother. He did not go more than a couple of yards from her.

"This awful stillness makes me unhappy," he said. "I want to hear the sound of the cowbells, the yelps of the collies, and the shouts of the herders."

Mother Reindeer watched him with kindly eyes. She was very proud of White Sox. He was her fifteenth fawn, and the smartest, handsomest, and most graceful and agile in the big herd.

He was very tall. His body was slender and well proportioned. His head was finely shaped and held very high; his horns were still in the velvet, and they were beautiful. His hair was of the darkest shade of brown — all except his legs, which, from the hoofs to the knees, were as white and smooth as the skin of a winter weasel, and his nose, which looked as if it had been dipped halfway to his eyes into a pail of milk.

Yes, indeed! Mother Reindeer had good reason to be proud of White Sox. He was strong as well as handsome; only a few hours after he was born he had been able to run with the other fawns and take care of himself. Now, at five months, he could outrun them all. And, strange as it may appear, all the other mothers in the big herd admitted that there was not another fawn to compare with White Sox.

Just at that moment, while Mother Reindeer was thinking about these things, a gentle breeze

"White Sox turned his nose in the same direction as hers, and sniffed, and sniffed, and sniffed."

from the northwest blew in her direction and kissed the tip of her nose. She sprang quickly to her feet. She stretched her graceful neck, lifted her upper lip slightly, and sniffed the breeze.

"What is it?" White Sox asked quickly. "Mother, do you scent the big herd?"

Mother Reindeer was nodding her head upward and downward. White Sox turned his nose in the same direction as hers, and sniffed, and sniffed, and sniffed.

"Come!" cried Mother Reindeer. "Let's be off!"

Away they went — right through the thick fog, just as if it had not been there at all. After they had gone a few miles, the heavy mist began to lift.

They could see a little farther, then still farther, and at last, on a low ridge straight ahead of them, White Sox caught sight of moving forms.

"Mother! Look, look! It's the big herd!" he shouted joyfully.

He was about to rush toward them, when his mother spoke.

"Not so fast, my son," she said. "That is a herd of caribou. They are our wild cousins."

White Sox was very much surprised. "Our wild cousins?" he repeated slowly. Then he became greatly excited. "Oh, mother, I'm so glad! I've always wanted to see our wild cousins. How lucky we are! Come, let's hurry!"

"No, no, my son! You have many lessons to learn," she said kindly. "Our wild cousins do not know we are coming to visit them. They have not scented us, because the wind is blowing from them to us. They will be startled when they see us. We must move very slowly. If we rush toward them, they will run away."

As White Sox and his mother moved toward the herd of white caribou, they left the last of the fog behind and could see their cousins quite plainly.

"They look exactly like us," said White Sox, after watching them for a little while.

"Look again, my son," said Mother Reindeer.

But at that moment the caribou caught sight of the strangers. They quickly bunched together, with heads erect, and watched them.

Mother Reindeer paused. White Sox stopped also.

"No, mother, I was wrong," he said. "I can see our cousins plainer now. Their bodies are more slender than those of the reindeer in our herd. Their legs and necks are longer. They hold their heads higher. There are no spotted or white ones among them."

"Very true," said Mother Reindeer. She liked to have White Sox find out things for himself. "The spotted and white ones are found only in the herds that live with man and serve him. Come, we will go to our wild cousins now. They are frightened. Walk very slowly, and pay attention to what I tell you."

"The caribou stood at attention as White Sox and his
mother came up to them."

II

A Taste of Wild Life

The caribou stood at attention as White Sox
and his mother came up to them. To White
Sox they seemed very shy and nervous, but he
supposed that was because they had not been
expecting company.

"Mother," he whispered, "why do they all
stare at me so?"

"You are the first white-legged and white-nosed
fawn they have ever seen," she told him. Then
she introduced him to them all.

White Sox held his head as high as theirs, but
he behaved very nicely while they admired his

beautiful markings. While his mother was greeting the older cousins, the younger ones gathered about him and invited him to join in their play. But White Sox was not in a playful mood. He was curious to learn more about these strange cousins; so he went back to his mother.

"Have you been here before, mother? " he asked. "Our wild cousins seem to know you quite well."

"Yes, my son. I have often made visits to the caribou at this time of the year," Mother Reindeer said. "But run away and eat your supper with the fawns. Keep your eyes and ears open, and learn all you can of their life and habits."

White Sox was very happy. This new world seemed a beautiful place to him. From the top of the ridge he could see for a long distance in every direction. Life was not a bit lonesome now. He skipped and frisked with the fawns, and ate his supper of moss with them in a tiny hollow just below the ridge where the big caribou were eating. Oh, it was the most delicious moss he had ever tasted! When sleeping time came, he went back to his mother, too tired and drowsy to say a word.

But do you suppose the wild caribou were going to allow the lazy fellow to sleep in peace? Not a bit of it! Four times during the night the herd changed its camping ground. White Sox was awakened out of a lovely nap each time in order to follow them.

But next day — well, he had forgotten this; and it was just as Mother Reindeer had expected it would be. The fawns had told him wonderful stories about their wild life. The newness and excitement of it had so charmed him that the foolish fellow wanted to stay with his wild cousins forever and ever.

Mother Reindeer was preparing for her afternoon nap. She had made herself comfortable on a nice soft bed of moss where she could see up the ridge and down the ridge, when White Sox came to her, all out of breath. He dropped down on the bed beside her without so much as asking her leave.

"Mother, I've changed my mind," he said, panting. "I don't want to go back to the big herd."

Mother Reindeer did not say a word. She wanted to know how much he had learned, and so she kept quiet till he had breath enough to tell her. She did not have to wait very long.

"I like this wild life, mother," he said. "Our cousins are free to come and go as they please. They eat on the mossy ranges in winter and on the grassy slopes in summer. They have sorrels and mushrooms, foliage of shrubs, and all kinds of dainties. The fawns are never robbed of their mothers' milk. They are never roped and thrown to the ground by cruel herders. They don't have their ears cut and their horns torn off."

White Sox was all out of breath again because he had talked so fast. He was quite excited, too.

"I've been thinking of my Cousin Bald Face," he went on. "If he had lived with the caribou, he would have been alive today. I shall never forget his death."

"Bald Face did not heed his mother's teaching, my son," said Mother Reindeer, gently.

"It wasn't his fault, mother. I had just been roped and thrown to the ground. One of the herders had taken two V's out of my right ear and another V out of my left ear — so you'd know I belonged to you, I suppose — when I saw the loop of the lasso close over Bald Face's left horn, near the end. The poor little fellow was running his fastest. The herder braced himself and held the lasso tight. My cousin's horn was pulled off. Oh, it was horrible! A piece of Bald Face's skull the size of my ear was torn off with the root of the horn, leaving his brain bare."

"The herder was a new one," said Mother Reindeer. "He had not learned his business. He will never injure another reindeer in that way. We must forgive him and try to forget it."

"Mother, I can't forget it," cried White Sox. "These wild cousins of ours can look forward to a long life of freedom and safety. They are not the slaves of herders and dogs. I want to stay with them."

"You are very young, my son. You have much to learn," said his mother.

"But I know what will happen to me if I stay with the big herd," he said. "I'll have to draw heavy sled loads in winter and carry tiresome packs in summer, if I am not killed by the butcher's knife when I am two years old. In that case the herders will eat my flesh and make clothing out of my hide. The skin of my white legs will be used for fancy boots for some herder."

Mother Reindeer nodded her head upward and downward. She knew the ways of the big herd and had seen these things happen many times. She knew that if her beautiful White Sox was intended for a sled deer, he would first have to be halter-broken. A herder would rope him and tie him to a piece of tundra surface that was higher than the rest of the tundra, called a "niggerhead." Then would follow the tedious work of breaking him to harness. He  would be a beast of burden in winter as long as his back-fat lasted. Back-fat is the fat that collects on a reindeer's back in summer, when there are green grass and shrubbery to eat. Reindeer moss alone does not give the reindeer strength enough for much hard work.

If White Sox was broken to harness, Mother Reindeer thought it quite likely that he would be selected by the mail carrier for that terrible journey of five hundred miles to

A herder.

"This wonderful fawn of hers might escape the butcher's knife and the herder's harness and be kept for a leader."

Kotzebue Sound. But she had reason to believe that, because of his perfect markings, this wonderful fawn of hers might escape the butcher's knife and the herder's harness and be kept for a leader of the big herd. It was because she thought this that she had brought him with her on a visit to the caribou.

"Mother," began White Sox, after thinking for a little while, "have you forgotten what Uncle Slim told us just before we became separated from the big herd?"

"No, indeed! But run away and play with the fawns now," she said. "Watch them carefully. You have not learned your lesson yet."

Mother Reindeer had intended to take a nap,

but she had many things to think of after White Sox left her. Uncle Slim had told them that probably the big herd would be pastured on the ice-coated sea beach during the coming winter. This meant that the sled deer would grow very thin again. The herders liked to pasture the herd there so that they could live in their old sod houses and be near the big village at Point Barrow.

Lack of moss would not be the only drawback; there was also the terror of the Eskimo dogs. Slim's brother had been crippled by a malamute dog, at Kivalina, when hauling mail on the Barrow-Kotzebue route. Last December, Slim and five other reindeer had been staked out for five nights near Point Barrow village. They were exposed to a fierce northeast wind while the drivers were enjoying themselves in the village, where feasting and dancing were going on. On the fifth night the wind had changed to the northwest, and the reindeer had been scented by hungry village dogs. After a desperate struggle, Slim and the other reindeer had broken their tethers and had outrun the dogs. They had run miles and miles back to the big herd, and so had saved their lives.

It was not all joy in the big herd. Mother Reindeer knew that very well. Many a time she too had been tempted to stay with her caribou cousins and adopt their free life. But always something had happened to make her change her mind. She felt sure it would be the same way with White Sox.

"'When I bent my head to take a drink, I saw the picture of my antlers.'"

III

White Sox Learns Many Things

When White Sox and the fawns returned from the brook where the dwarf willows grew, he was full of a new subject that he could not understand, and of course he wanted his mother to explain it.

"Mother," he said, "the water in the brook was very clear this morning. When I bent my head to take a drink, I saw the picture of my antlers. They are not so big and strong as those of the caribou fawns. There is one little fellow here — much younger than I — whose upright branches are longer than mine."[1]

[1] The October antlers of the barren-ground caribou fawns of the interior of Alaska are shorter than those of the fawns of reindeer. Many

"Very likely he'll need his horns more than you will," said Mother Reindeer.

"Not if I become a caribou, mother; and I do so want to stay here and have a good time all my life," pleaded White Sox. Then he looked at her curiously and said, "Mother, the caribou all seem to have better antlers than the reindeer. You are like the caribou; your coat is of the same color when you stand in the deep moss and hide your white ankles. But your antlers — "

"Well, what's the matter with them?" she asked, when her son paused.

"I don't know, mother," he answered. "Something seems to be wrong with them. You have twenty-two points still covered with velvet, but the points are soft. They curve inward. I don't think they would be of much use in a fight."

"Neither do I," said Mother Reindeer, "but I am not expecting to get into a fight. I lost a set of beautiful antlers when you were born. Mothers usually lose their horns at such times. The big herd was kept on the shores of a lagoon near the beach while my new set was growing. Mosquitoes were very thick at that place. I had to keep shaking my head from side to side to beat off the pests. That constant striking of my growing horns caused them to curve inward at the ends."

"The leader of the caribou has a fine set of antlers," White Sox told her. "I counted forty-

of them are stubs only 4 or 5 inches long. Those of the reindeer fawns are from 8 to 14 inches in length.

seven points, all peeled and sharpened for service. Will mine ever be like his, mother?"

"Don't worry, my son," said Mother Reindeer, kindly. "You'll grow a new set of antlers each year. I've grown and cast fifteen sets. No two of them were alike."

Mother Reindeer knew that the size and shape of antlers and the number of their points all depended on the summer range. If she and White Sox were to adopt the wild life of the caribou, their antlers would be as large and strong as those of their wild cousins. But she was too wise to tell this to her son before he had learned his first lessons.

Away he skipped. If he could not match the caribou fawns in antlers, he could equal them in fleetness. My, how he could run! Mother Reindeer watched him now, and she thought that his white stockings looked for all the world like a streak of snow above the moss. She knew, too, that his cousins envied him those white stockings, and she hoped that he would have sense enough not to become vain of them.

When the second night came, White Sox was very tired and sleepy. But his wild cousins would not let him rest in peace. Just about midnight they decided to move to the next ridge. They were no sooner comfortably settled there than the leader ordered them all to another place. When daylight came, White Sox complained to his mother about this frequent moving.

"Mother, do our wild cousins never rest and sleep?" he asked. "I've lost more sleep these two nights than during all the past month. And tell me, please, mother, why do they eat the poor, short dry moss on the top of the ridges and knob hills, when there is much better grazing in the valleys?"

But Mother Reindeer answered only with a shake of her wise head. She knew perfectly well that White Sox might forget the things she told him, but he would always remember the things he found out for himself.

While White Sox waited for her to speak, he saw her turn her head to the right, then to the left, just as the caribou were always doing — looking for trouble.

"Mother, you've caught their nervous habit," he said. "It's the only thing about our cousins that I don't like. Well, if I can't get enough sleep here, I'm surely going to have enough to eat. I'm not going to punish myself by adopting foolish caribou habits. There'll be some good moss in that little valley down there. I'm going to have it for my breakfast."

Away he went. Mother Reindeer followed him quickly. Sure enough, as they crossed a patch where dwarf willows grew they came upon some of the finest moss. Um! it made their mouths water. But do you think White Sox had that moss for his breakfast? No, indeed!

Mother Reindeer shook her head. "You come

right up to this other knoll at once," she ordered,
sternly. "The restless habits of your wild cousins
are not foolish styles, as you'll soon find out.
Come right along, now, and pay attention to
what I say. Your father once called my ear but-
tons a 'foolish female style,' but he changed his
mind about it when the herders clamped but-
tons on his own ears."

White Sox followed his mother up the slope to
the little knoll. He did not like it one bit, but
he dared not disobey her. They had barely
reached the high ground when they heard the
frightened squawkings of a flock of ptarmigan,
which rose like a cloud out of another patch of
low arctic willows a few hundred yards from the
spot where they had crossed the little valley.

"Look, look!" exclaimed White Sox, becoming
excited. "I never saw so many ptarmigan before.
I believe there are as many as there are reindeer
in our big herd."

But Mother Reindeer was looking this way and
that, this way and that, looking and listening,
just as the caribou did.

"Mother!" shouted White Sox, suddenly, "look
at our wild cousins on that other ridge! See how
scared they are! Ptarmigan can't hurt them."

"Keep quiet, my son!" commanded his mother.
"That squawking of the ptarmigan is a danger
signal. There's a hungry fox among the willows
who wanted to make his breakfast off a fat
ptarmigan, or else it is —"

"The very next instant a big black wolf came out of the
willows."

"What, mother?"

White Sox had crept close to her side; but he
also was looking this way and that, this way and
that.

"It may be a wolf," said Mother Reindeer.

"A wolf!" repeated White Sox, in a whisper.

"If it were a herder looking for us, we should
see his head and shoulders above the willows.
It must be that a wolf has scented us from afar."

Mother Reindeer was right. But it was not
one wolf. Hardly had she said the words when
three big gray wolves left the willows by a small
ravine that ended near the herd of frightened
caribou.

But the caribou could not see the wolves. White Sox forgot everything except the fact that his cousins were in danger. He must warn them instantly.

Before his mother could stop him, he had given out three piercing bleats, "*He-awk! he-awk! he-awk!*"

The very next instant a big black wolf came out of the willows. It was followed by a gray one. They started up the slope toward him and his mother.

"At her heels went White Sox, terribly scared."

IV

A RACE FOR LIFE

"There! You've done it!" exclaimed Mother Reindeer. "Come on! Keep right in my tracks and don't turn your head to the right or left. Do exactly as I do!"

Down the mossy slope she started at her swiftest speed. At her heels went White Sox, terribly scared, and thankful that he could run so fast.

For a long time he thought of nothing but getting away from the fierce wolves. Then he remembered his cousins. He wondered if they had heard his signal, if they too were running for their lives.

Away off — some three miles ahead — Mother Reindeer had spied a lake, shaped like an hourglass. She was making for this lake as fast as her feet could carry her. Not once did she look back to see where the wolves were.

To White Sox the lake looked like two patches of water connected by a narrow neck. He was thinking as he ran, wondering if his mother would take him into one of these pieces of water, and if the wolves would keep them there until the water froze over. He had been in icy water once. Some Eskimo dogs had chased him and his uncle into the Arctic Ocean in July, and had kept them there until a herder came and drove the dogs away. His uncle had told him that lakes and streams would soon begin to freeze; so he knew.

White Sox forgot his mother's command and looked back. He had never heard of Lot's wife and the pillar of salt. My! How his heart beat when he saw the two wolves behind him! He was just going to urge his mother to greater speed, when his attention was called to something else.

They were entering a grassy bog. Mother Reindeer was slowing down to a trot and heading toward the narrow neck between the two lakes.

At first White Sox was too much surprised to speak. "It looks as if it weren't very deep, mother," he called warningly. "Let's make for the deepest water. Uncle Slim told me that wolves can't swim very well in deep water."

His uncle had also told him that if wolves or dogs followed them into deep water, reindeer could strike out with their hoofs and drown their enemies. But White Sox was too much out of breath to explain all that to his mother just at the moment.

But, bless your heart! Old Mother Reindeer knew all those things, and much more.

"Save your breath, White Sox!" she said sternly. "Follow me closely and do exactly as I do."

Then, instead of hurrying, she went slower and slower.

White Sox was too much scared to think. He followed right in his mother's tracks, getting as close to her as he could, for he could hear the whining yips of the wolves behind him.

They had now reached the shore of the narrow neck between the lakes. Instead of jumping in and dashing across, Mother Reindeer began to walk, slowly and very carefully.

"Huh! huh! huh!"

It was the hard breathing of the fierce wolves close behind White Sox. He was terribly afraid their fangs would be nipping his hind legs in about a minute. He made up his mind to bound past his mother and reach the farther shore ahead of her.

But, oh my! It was lucky he did not.

That narrow neck was a slough. The water in it was not water at all. The minute he put his foot in that thick, gummy, smelly oil, White Sox knew why his mother had slowed down. It reached up to his mother's knees, and was so sticky that he could hardly wade through it. He followed her meekly, with slow and careful steps.

The slough was about twelve yards across.[1] Halfway over, White Sox looked back again. The two wolves had just reached the brink of the slough.

In they plunged, together, in too great a hurry to notice the resinous substance. But two jumps were enough for them. The oil splashed over their sides and backs. Their great tails became heavy with it, so heavy that they could hardly lift them. They turned slowly and waddled back to the shore in a terrible mess. There was no breakfast of reindeer meat for them that morning.

Mother Reindeer and White Sox reached the farther shore and stepped out of the slough. They stamped their feet to shake off the sticky stuff, but they couldn't get rid of it.

Poor White Sox! His beautiful stockings were dyed a rich black color.

"We are like the caribou now, mother," he said sorrowfully.

"Never mind. It will come off when we shed our hair next July," Mother Reindeer told him.

[1] These oil lakes were discovered near the Arctic coast east of Point Barrow a few years ago. In the fall of 1921 they were staked by two oil companies.

"There were no lame ones and no old ones. Now I know the reason. The wolves caught and ate them."

White Sox was so thankful at having escaped the wolves that he did not waste much time in regrets. He had learned a lesson that morning that he would never forget.

"Mother, you are the most wonderful reindeer in all the world," he said proudly. "But why didn't you tell me of your plan of escape?"

"There was no time, my son. Besides, fawns learn best by seeing and doing."

"Would the wolves have gone into that shallow oil slough if we had not held back until they almost caught us?"

"Certainly not! The wolf is the greediest and most destructive of all our enemies," Mother Reindeer said. "We can only defeat him when we outwit him and lead him into a trap."

"I see!" cried White Sox. "If you had not tempted them to follow us across the sticky slough, they would have gone around one of the lakes and would still be chasing us. They cannot chase us now; their coats are too heavy. Look at them, mother! They waddle like the porcupines in the timbered country that Uncle Slim told us about. Where is the timbered country?"

"It's about ten days' journey south of here," Mother Reindeer told him. Then she asked him if he still wished to live with the wild caribou.

"No, no, mother! There were no lame ones and no old ones among our wild cousins. I wondered about it yesterday, but now I know the reason. The wolves caught and ate them."

"Now do you know," Mother Reindeer asked him, "why our wild cousins are always looking this way and that?"

"Yes," White Sox answered, "I know now. It's the wolves. They are always on the lookout for wolves. They dare not sleep at night for fear of these enemies. They dare not even graze in the willow valleys where the best moss grows. They must have strong, sharp antlers with which to protect themselves. I understand it all now, mother. Our wild cousins must ever be on the watch for these sneaking wolves. No, mother! No wild caribou life for me! Let us go back to the tame life of the big herd."

"Mother Reindeer changed her course so that they almost
faced the wind."

V

White Sox Travels through a Blizzard

White Sox did not ask if his mother knew the
way back to the big herd. He had learned his
lesson well. Besides, Mother Reindeer had told
him that it was not the first time she had visited
the caribou. When she said, "Come, let us be
off!" he was quite ready to follow without asking
foolish questions.

Away they went at a brisk trot. Both were
glad to be going home. Presently Mother Reindeer said, "If all goes well, we should reach the
big herd by tomorrow night. I have a story to
tell you before we get there. All reindeer mothers
tell this story to their fawns."

28

Mother Reindeer would have told this story to White Sox long ago, but she had wanted him to meet his wild cousins first. White Sox was different from the other fawns, and — well, you'll understand after you have heard the story.

They had traveled about ten miles when a northwest breeze sprang up. The air soon became full of flying snow. Mother Reindeer changed her course so that they almost faced the wind. It was a terrible wind. White Sox had never faced a blizzard before. He kept close in on his mother's side, and he snuggled his head to her shoulder. In this way they trotted along at about six miles an hour.

The air became colder and colder. Soon the snow was like the fog — it walled them in as they ran. Mother Reindeer did not slacken her speed, and White Sox felt quite sure it was all right. But after they had gone about twenty-four miles, he began to feel very tired and hungry.

"Please let us stop and eat a bit of moss," he begged. "We didn't finish our breakfast, mother. I want to rest awhile."

"Not yet, my son," Mother Reindeer said. "A little farther on, when we reach the other side of that ridge, we shall be out of the storm zone. Then we will rest and eat."

White Sox thought those last three miles were the longest he had ever run in his life. He had never, never been quite so hungry. But on they went, and at last the ridge was crossed. There was nice weather then. And right there on the slope, under three inches of freshly fallen snow, was a bed of moss. Um! It was the nicest moss White Sox had ever tasted.

"Is it because I am so hungry, or because of the snow, that this moss is so good?" he asked his mother.

"Both, my son," she replied. "In summer, moss is either too dry or too wet. We eat a little of it, but we like the grass and foliage better. These produce our back-fat, which we must have to help us through the winter. Snow gives the moss the right amount of moisture. We live on it through the long winter, but every moon we lose some of our back-fat. We are always glad when the snow goes and the grass comes."

"Mother, what is the starvation moon?" White Sox asked, after they had eaten awhile in silence. "I have heard Uncle Slim speak of it."

"That is a spring moon," said Mother Reindeer, and then she explained all about it. "When the herd is kept too near the sea beach and the snow is deep and hard, reindeer become very poor and weak. They have to dig through the snow for all their meals, and there isn't much to eat after all their digging. Some reindeer mothers are so poor when their fawns come that until the grass grows they don't have milk enough for them. There was a starvation moon after your sister was born, and consequently her growth was stunted. Luckily for you, last winter and

"'Your mother was in good condition, and you grew fast and strong.'"

spring were what is called 'open.' The herders moved the herd back a day's journey each moon. Your mother was in good condition and had plenty of milk. You grew fast and strong."

White Sox nibbled awhile; then he thought of something else that he wanted to know.

"Mother, why did we change our course and go almost directly against the wind when we were traveling through that blizzard?" he asked.

"That was to protect ourselves from the driving blast and from wolves," said Mother Reindeer. "Don't you know that our hair slants backward like the feathers of a duck? A driving wind that strikes us from behind or on the side gets under our hair and chills us."

"When we face the wind we can scent wolves and Eskimo dogs ahead of us. But then wolves behind us can scent us, can't they, mother?"

"Yes, my son; but no wolf or dog can face a blizzard like the snowstorm we passed through today and overtake a reindeer or a caribou. Our enemies like to scent us, or see us, and then sneak up as they tried to do this morning. Our wild cousins are in the greatest danger when they are resting."

"Resting!" exclaimed White Sox. "Why, mother, our poor cousins don't know what rest is! But tell me, please, when the snowflakes became hard sleet today, didn't they hurt your eyes?"

"No, my son. I held my head down in such a way that one of my branches sheltered my left eye most of the time. My right eye was protected by the broad shovel prong over my nose. I could close my left eye to rest it while running. Even when we have no horns, we can close one eye and turn our head so as to protect the other. Until you have learned this trick, you must always crowd in on the lee side of a big reindeer for protection when in a blizzard."

"I'll remember that, mother. But I'm very sleepy now. May I rest awhile?"

"Yes. We'll go to the top of that little knoll over yonder. You may sleep while I am chewing my cud."

When they had reached the place, Mother

Reindeer selected a nice bed of moss covered with a clean sheet of freshly fallen snow. They needed no blankets other than their thick, warm coats. In about two minutes White Sox was fast asleep.

"And under the bright arctic moon, there on the very top of
the continent, she told him the story."

VI

Under the Arctic Moon

I<small>F</small> you wish to know where White Sox was sleeping, you must get your geography and turn to
the map of Alaska. Now find the seventy-first
parallel. North of that you will notice a little
point of land jutting out into the Arctic Ocean,
called Point Barrow. Just southwest of that
point is Barrow, the village to which the big herd
belonged.

The little knoll where White Sox was sleeping
was on the seventy-first parallel, away up at the
top of the North American continent. The
freshly fallen snow stretched eastward and west-

ward, northward and southward, from this little knoll; in fact, it covered all the land from the seventieth parallel to the Arctic Ocean. But White Sox knew nothing about parallels and such things. To him that arctic land was the whole world.

Mother Reindeer knew a lot more than that. She was seventeen years old. She had seen and heard so much that she was very wise.

When White Sox waked from his nap, he thought it was daylight. The brightness dazzled him. He winked his eyes and looked about him. A great big arctic moon was shining down upon him. What a beautiful moon it was! And how the snow glistened and shone! He winked his eyes several times; then he looked for his mother.

She was pawing through the snow near him to get moss for her midnight lunch.

"Mother, this is the whitest world I've ever seen," he said. Then he sprang up and began to dig moss for himself, for he was hungry again.

A light breeze was blowing from the north-west, and the air was much colder. White Sox rubbed his face against his mother's shoulder to brush the frost from his eyes and nose. Then he took a mouthful of moss and looked about him.

There was not a living thing to be seen. Yes, there was! A great arctic owl was perched on a little mound not very far away.

"Mother, are owls as wise as they look?" White Sox asked. He took another bite of moss.

"'He swoops down to catch his own supper and meets his finish in the sharp claws and teeth of the lynx.'"

"No, not always," Mother Reindeer answered, "but sometimes they are cunning enough to outwit sleepy reindeer mothers and kill their new-born fawns."

"Do the owls ever get caught by our other enemies?"

"Sometimes. Among our lesser enemies the lynx is said to be wiser than the wisest owl. The lynx eats rabbits, mice, and birds. He studies the habits of these creatures. He knows that the owl is always watching to swoop down on some helpless field mouse. My own mother told me that when a lynx is hungry for owl meat, he will burrow in well-packed snow, leaving a small opening in the crust about the size of your tail. He then lies on his back in his snow cave and pokes his short bobtail through the roof and wags it to and fro. When the owl sees it, he thinks it is a field mouse. He swoops down to catch his own supper and meets his finish in the sharp claws and teeth of the lynx."

"The lynx are more cunning than the wolves. Do you fear them as much, mother?"

"No, my son. When they attack our kind, it is usually a weak fawn or an injured reindeer."

"Mother, that little caribou cousin of mine — the fawn with the big antlers — couldn't run very fast. Do you think the wolves would catch him?" White Sox now asked.

"It's quite likely they would," said Mother Reindeer. "The weaklings always go first to feed our enemies, and their going helps to save the strong ones. A wild caribou can never hope to die a natural death. Our wild cousins know that at some time or other they must be caught and eaten by their enemies. Their freedom, which appeared so attractive to you, is dangerous and deprives them of protection. Even when some of their number are always on watch, prowling enemies will take them by surprise, as they did yesterday."

"Mother," said White Sox, thoughtfully, "knowing this, why didn't one of us stand watch while the other slept?"

"One of us did," she answered. "I slept the

'caribou sleep,' half a minute on and half a minute off, while you slept the reindeer sleep.''

White Sox was greatly surprised when he heard this. He felt that he had been very thoughtless and selfish. "You should have let me do my share of watching," he said.

"You were too tired, my son," his mother told him. "Besides, you knew nothing about the ways of caribou and wolves before we came on this visit to our cousins. In the big herd the reindeer sleep long and sound; they have no fear of enemies. The Eskimo herders and the collies watch over them. Cowbells frighten the wolves and scare them away."

"Yes, mother, I understand that now. Reindeer life is much safer than caribou life, but — "

"But what?"

White Sox seemed to be puzzled about something. He thought about it for a minute, and then he said, "Mother, you never said a word when the herders killed my two big brothers. Did you think it right?"

Mother Reindeer did not speak, but she nodded her head upward and downward, very slowly.

"They killed two of my uncles also," continued White Sox, "but they never touched my sisters or my aunts. And now I come to think of it, mother, it is always the brothers and uncles that are killed. Are we born to be eaten?"

Mother Reindeer looked very serious. "It is time I told you the big story," she said. "After you have heard it you will understand many things that seem strange to you now. Come, if you've finished your meal. Lie here by my side. No wolves can surprise us on this knoll. The beautiful moon is our friend. I am going to tell you how the first wild caribou was tamed and became a reindeer."

After they had made themselves comfortable, Mother Reindeer said, "First I must tell you that it will be a white world for seven moons. From now until we shed our coats next summer, you may be known in the big herd as 'Black Sox'!"

Poor White Sox! He looked sadly at his dark stockings, which were almost as black as the feathers of a raven; but he answered thoughtfully: "I am thankful my nose is still white. But I am not worrying about my name and color. I want to hear the story of how the first caribou was tamed, mother."

This pleased Mother Reindeer very much. "Good, my son!" she said. "Now for the story!"

And under the bright arctic moon, on the very top of the great American continent, she told him the story.

"'He was the first caribou that ever had any white markings.'"

VII

Mother Reindeer's Story of White Feet

"Ever and ever so long ago, on a fine summer day, a great herd of wild caribou was browsing near the seashore," said Mother Reindeer. "This shore was far away toward the setting sun, across the great piece of water. There were no reindeer at the time of which I am speaking. This herd of caribou was more than ten times as large as our own big herd. There were so many of them, and they were so strong, that they had grown careless.

"Wolves did not usually bother the caribou in summer. There had been no hunters chasing

them for a long time. The great herd felt quite
safe. It was their custom to keep a few hundred
of their swiftest runners on picket duty all around
the herd, to watch for enemies. But, as I have
just told you, they had grown careless.

"In this great herd of wild caribou was a fawn
with white legs and white nose. He was the
first caribou that ever had any white markings.
All the others were very proud of him. They
named him 'White Feet.'"

"Did I look like him, mother?" asked White
Sox, who was much interested in the story.

"Yes, indeed! You were exactly like him in
every way, my son," said Mother Reindeer,
proudly. "The fame of this first marked fawn
spread far and wide. Many other bands of caribou came to see him. They all agreed that he
was born to be king of the caribou. So much attention caused his mother to be very careful to
train him in the right way. He had many, many
things to learn."

"Yes, mother. A fawn who is going to be a
great leader must know more than the other reindeer fawns," said White Sox.

Mother Reindeer was much pleased at the interest her son was taking in the story. "That
is very true," she said. "White Feet was very ob-
serving and thoughtful. He became wise while he
was a fawn. He remembered what his mother told
him. He often thought about it and planned what
he would do when he grew up to be the leader.

"Now, as I told you before, this great herd of wild caribou felt a little too safe. One fine summer day, when they were grazing near the shore, a large band of hungry wolves scented them. These crafty enemies came nearer and nearer without the herd's knowing anything about them. At last, when they thought they were close enough, out they rushed. The terrified herd of caribou stampeded pell-mell into the icy water of the Arctic Ocean."

"Oh!" gasped White Sox. "Did the wolves get many of them?"

"Wait and listen," said Mother Reindeer. "White Feet and six other young fawns who always followed him had gone up on a hill to the right of the great herd. They were not caught in the stampede, but they were cut off from the herd. A large band of fierce wolves was between them and the caribou. All the fawns except young White Feet were very much frightened. They began to 'mill,' or run around in a circle. White Feet remembered what his mother had told him about wolves. He was only half your age, but he took command of the little band of fawns and led them down the other side of the hill, across a narrow valley, and then up the side of a high ridge. He planned to get over the summit and out of sight before any of the wolves began to look for stragglers.

"When they reached the top of the ridge, they could see the herd swimming about in the

water.   The many antlers looked like a great
mass of brushwood afloat.   And they could see
the wolves pacing up and down along the shore,
either too cowardly or too wise to follow the caribou into the water.

"The fawns stood on the high ridge, their
mouths wide open.   Great drops of perspiration
fell from their lolling tongues.   Young White
Feet was wondering how long the wolves would
keep the caribou in the icy water, and how he
could lead his little band back to their mothers.
He looked all about him, this way and that,
and what do you think he saw?

"Three big gray wolves were creeping up the
side of the ridge, coming straight toward him and
the fawns."

"Oh!" cried White Sox, greatly excited.   "What
did he do, mother?"

"He told the fawns to follow him and to do
just as he did," said Mother Reindeer.   "He had
seen a small bay farther along the beach.   It
was made by a long, narrow spit of land that curved
like the main branch of my antlers.   'Come on!'
he cried.   'It's a race for life to that little bay
down yonder.'

"Then away he went, with the other six fawns
at his heels.   Down, down, down toward the bay
they raced.   When they were about halfway there,
White Feet saw smoke ahead.   It was coming
from a skin tent that lay between them and
the bay."

"'Then, just as the first wolf was about to seize the hindermost fawn, he and his little band swerved to one side and burst into the big tent.'"

"Oh, a herder's tent!" cried White Sox.

"No, indeed!" said Mother Reindeer. "There were no herders in those days, my son. It was the tent of a hunter. White Feet didn't know which was the more to be feared, a wolf or a hunter. Both were the enemies of the caribou. And the little band of fawns were depending on him to lead them to safety."

"I understand," said White Sox. "A leader must decide things for himself, and do it quickly. He can't ask his mother every time he faces a duty."

"Yes," said Mother Reindeer, "and the three gray wolves forced White Feet to decide quickly this time. They were coming down the slope behind the fawns. White Feet knew that the wolves were gaining on them, but as he looked ahead, he saw that the tent flap was open. He felt quite sure that his little band could not reach the bay, and he had been told that wolves would avoid a hunter's tent in daylight. But these beasts thought they were surely going to have a big feed of fawn meat.

"White Feet shouted to his followers to turn and dash into the tent. Then, just as the first wolf was about to seize the hindermost fawn, he and his little band swerved to one side and burst into the big tent.

"Whiz! whiz! whiz!

"The native hunter, all unknown to the fawns and wolves, had been watching the race from behind the tent. Three gray wolves now lay on the ground outside, pinned fast by the hunter's terrible arrows."

"Oh, mother, mother!" cried White Sox, who was trembling with excitement. "Did the hunter kill White Feet and his six fawns?"

Mother Reindeer looked at her son for a moment in silence and then continued her story.

"'A woman and her three children squatted near the fire.'"

VIII

The First Human Friend

"Inside the big tent," Mother Reindeer went on, "a woman and her three children squatted near the fire. They were eating a freshly cooked duck. They were so taken by surprise when the little band of caribou fawns dashed in through their open tent flap that at first they could not speak or move. Then the mother sprang up and fastened the tent flap tight.

"White Feet and his followers had come to a stop at the farther side of the tent. They stood bunched together, with heads erect. All but White Feet were shaking with fear. They had seen the woman close the tent flap. They knew that they were prisoners now, and they thought that they had escaped one death only to meet another. Then they saw the tent flap open a little way. The hunter peeped in; then he opened it wider, slipped inside the tent, and closed the flap quickly.

"White Feet noticed that the hunter carried his big bow in his hand. He noticed also that he and his family all wore clothes made of caribou skins. They spoke to each other in strange sounds such as the fawns had never before heard. They all appeared to be very much excited and pleased. They looked at the fawns, and the fawns looked at them.

"Suddenly the bigger boy gave a loud cry and pointed at White Feet. The hunter and the others looked at White Feet, too. Then they talked in excited tones.

"White Feet, of course, didn't know what they were saying, but he felt quite sure that they were talking about his white markings. Oh, how he wished his mother had been with him! Then he remembered that a leader must not think of himself when others depend on him. Here were the six poor little fawns scared half to death, and he had promised to take care of them. What should he do?

"He looked at the bigger boy, and the bigger boy looked at him. There was something in the boy's eyes that gave White Feet courage. He didn't seem like an enemy. He stood near his father, but his head came only as high as the hunter's elbow.

"White Feet made up his mind to trust this boy. Then he did the boldest thing ever done by a caribou. He walked across the tent to where the bigger boy stood and rubbed his head against the boy's arm."

"Oh!" gasped White Sox. "How brave he was!"

"Yes," said Mother Reindeer, "that little caribou fawn was the first of his kind to try to make friends with an enemy. Of course the boy was surprised. He touched White Feet on the head. He spoke kindly to him and patted his shoulder. All the others stopped talking and watched them.

"The bigger boy stooped down and stroked White Feet's beautiful stockings. White Feet rubbed his head against the boy's arm again and tried to tell him how much he wanted him for a friend.

"The boy's young sister wanted to touch the fawn's pretty stockings. She was a little bit afraid. She moved close beside the bigger boy, put out her hand very carefully, and just touched the top of the nearest white stocking. Then she laughed, and the two boys laughed, and their mother laughed. And what do you think White Feet did?

"*He kissed that little girl.* Yes, he did — right on the cheek. He licked her cheek with his warm tongue.

"The little girl wasn't a bit afraid of him after that. She stroked his white stockings, talked baby talk to him, and then she put her arms about his neck and loved him.

"White Feet felt pretty sure that the children would not let the hunter kill him — just then. But he had to think for Blackie — the other male fawn of his little band — and the five does. He told Blackie and the doe fawns to make friends with the other boy and his mother. At first they were too scared to move, but at last poor Blackie got courage enough to walk up to the younger boy and rub his head against his arm. This seemed to please the younger boy very much. Before long all the doe fawns had followed his example, and the human beings were laughing and talking kindly to them.

"The hunter had been shaking his head, but now he nodded it upward and downward. White Feet felt sure that he was saying 'yes' to what the children had been asking, and that none of the little band would be killed at once. White Feet watched the hunter very carefully, but he kept close to the bigger boy because the boy was his first friend.

"After a little while the hunter made two small halters of sealskin rope. He put one over White Feet's head and the other over Blackie's. Then the bigger boy led White Feet out of the tent and on to the narrow spit. The younger boy led Blackie. The five doe fawns followed them, and so did the little girl and her mother and father.

"'Dainten and White Feet loved each other.'"

"When they were all far out on the spit, the hunter stretched his fish net across the narrow neck of ground. White Feet and his band were now prisoners on the spit. They were very glad to be alive and safe from the wolves. They didn't know how long the hunter would let them live, and oh! how they did want their mothers! But they were very hungry too, and when White Feet saw some nice grass and scrubby willows, you may be quite sure that the little band forgot their troubles and ate a good supper.

"Afterward White Feet examined the long, narrow spit. It was low and rolling, and most of it was covered with moss and grass. There were dwarf willows too, and along its western shore, under a long bluff, was a level drift of old winter snow. The place looked mighty good to White Feet, especially when he found that the children were going to live on the sand spit with them. That very night the hunter and his family moved their tent inside the fish-net corral. The little band of fawns had a long sleep in perfect safety.

"Next day the hunter and his wife stood and watched the fawns play with the children. The hunter seemed to be most interested in White Feet. When he spoke to him, White Feet would go right up to the hunter and rub his head against the man's arm or leg. You see, White Feet had thought it all out and decided that the band must have the hunter for a friend; then their lives would be safe. But of course the hunter didn't know that. He was very much puzzled. He stared at White Feet and talked to him as if the fawn with the unheard-of markings were the, returned spirit of his dead father, who had been a chief and a mighty hunter. After a few days the hunter went away.

"The captive fawns soon forgot their sorrow and fear. The spit was a safe home. They had a variety of forage and plenty of it. They had loving companions. They could sleep soundly without fear of enemies. It was a new life to them and they liked it.

"The bigger boy's name was Dainten. White Feet soon discovered that. The two were together nearly all the time. They loved each other.

"But White Feet always remembered that the hunter and his family dressed in caribou skins. This made him very thoughtful. He felt quite sure that if all his followers were allowed to live and grow up, they must find a way to be of use to the hunter."

"'White Feet smelled at them, but he couldn't make out what Dainten intended to do.'"

IX

White Feet Finds a Way of Serving Man

"One day," continued Mother Reindeer, "some driftwood was washed up by the sea. Dainten pulled the pieces up on the beach. He found two that were crooked near the end. These pieces were of the same length, and the crooked ends were bent in about the same way.

"White Feet smelled at them, but he couldn't make out what Dainten intended to do as he watched him place the two pieces side by side, a short distance apart. Dainten then took some shorter pieces of driftwood, placed them crosswise on the others, and lashed them fast with sealskin thongs.

53

It was a strange-looking thing he had made. The crooked ends bent upward. To the cross-piece nearest these he fastened a stout rope of sealskin thongs. He then placed his little sister and brother on the thing and pulled them over the snow."

"I know!" exclaimed White Sox, quickly. "That was a sled."

"It was," said Mother Reindeer. "White Feet stood and watched them use the sled. He was doing some hard thinking. He wanted to do everything he saw Dainten do. When the bigger boy had given his little brother and sister one ride, White Feet asked Dainten to let him draw the sled. Of course Dainten didn't know what White Feet was saying; but when White Feet put his neck under the rope and tried to take his place in front of the sled, Dainten began to understand.

"He laughed and patted White Feet. He put the rope around his neck and tied it so it would not slip and choke him. Then he tied a small piece of rope to the right side of the halter band that White Feet was still wearing, and another piece to the left side. It was the hour after sunset. The snow, which had been soft and mushy at noon, was now hard and crusted.

"Dainten took his place on the front end of the sled and held the lines in his hands. His sister and brother sat behind him. When all was ready, he gave a slap of the lines on the fawn's sides.

"'To prevent its running against his heels, he swerved to the
left, giving the riders a great spill.'"

White Feet understood. He started very slowly and carefully, but he found that the loaded sled was easy to draw over the trail of hard snow. When Dainten urged him to go faster, he broke into a trot. All the other fawns joined the party. It was wonderful fun.

"On their return to the starting place, Dainten thought he would see how fast they could go. He gave a harder slap of the lines. Away they went down the gentle slope. The snow from the hind hoofs of White Feet hit their faces and made the children laugh. How glad they were, and how happy! And how proud White Feet was to be of service to them!

"They were going so fast as they neared the bottom of the slope that White Feet could not keep ahead of the sled. To prevent its running against his heels, he swerved to the left, giving the riders a great spill."

"Mother, that's a wonderful story!" cried White Sox. "That was the first sled reindeer, the first reindeer harness, the first reindeer ride, and the first spill!"

"Yes, my son," said Mother Reindeer, "the very first. It was the beginning of a new kind of service to man. As I told you before, the hunter was away. He came home while the children were sledding on the snow. He stepped from his boat and watched them in great surprise. And oh, how he laughed when the sled upset! He patted White Feet and spoke kindly to him, and he nodded his head upward and downward several times. Then he put the harness on Blackie and tied him in front of the little sled.

"White Feet told Blackie to watch for the signal and go very carefully. Dainten's brother drove him. Blackie did good work. You see, he had watched White Feet and had learned how to do as he did. Dainten's brother was very proud of Blackie.

"After a while the hunter went to his boat. All the children and the fawns followed him to see what he had brought from his hunting trip. First he took out a lot of ducks, some geese, and a swan. Then he unloaded a great many brown and white ptarmigan. His wife was much pleased when she saw that he had brought her two hair seals. She and the children carried the birds and dragged the seals up to the tent. But the fawns didn't follow then. The hunter was pulling some fresh caribou skins out of his boat."

"Oh!" cried White Sox, in excitement.

"Yes," said Mother Reindeer, "and the very first skin White Feet smelled at was his own mother's. The neck and hind legs were all chewed up by the teeth of wolves. Of course he felt very badly about it. The world seemed a lonely place to him after losing his mother. But he knew again that a leader must not think of himself. He smelled at the other skins. They all showed the teeth marks of wolves, and all of them were the skins of old mothers.

"White Feet knew that the old mothers were usually the weaklings of the herd. Their death saved many fawns from being caught. Then it came to White Feet that the death of these mothers might be the means of saving his own little band of fawns. The hunter and his family would now have plenty of caribou skins for the coming winter. They would not need his and Blackie's and those of the doe fawns.

"It was while White Feet was smelling at the skins that Dainten returned from the tent. The boy stood beside White Feet and looked at him, just for all the world as if he understood that the poor torn skin had belonged to White Feet's mother. From that minute Dainten and White Feet became lifelong friends. Dainten patted the fawn and tried to comfort him. To White Feet a human being had taken the place of his own dear old mother.

"Later, the hunter helped the boys make better harness for White Feet and Blackie. It was the kind now used by our herders. Instead of the curved piece of wood for each shoulder, he used a strap of sealskin about as broad as your ear, placing it over the left shoulder and neck and between the fore legs. The two ends of this band were fastened to the end of the single trace, back of the right fore leg, where they passed under the belly band. The trace stretched from the ends of the collar band to the sled, outside of the right hind leg.

"With these harnesses the hunter trained White Feet and Blackie to work together. He was well pleased with them and sent his five dogs to his brother, who lived a day's journey down the beach. The hunter knew that it would require much of the dried meat he had put up through the summer to feed his team dogs through the winter. His new sled deer didn't eat meat. That meant less work for the hunter and his wife.

"Of course the hunter was anxious to try out these sled deer with a heavy load. Luckily for White Feet and Blackie, their muscles were hard and strong by the time the first new snow came. They had plenty of back-fat too. All their work had been but play, but now they were to be of real service to man. The hunter's supplies, gathered during the summer, must be moved from the spit to a small grove of alders a day's journey inland. This was the hunter's winter home."

The first load hauled by White Feet and Blackie.

X

The Hunter Becomes a Herder

"The first load hauled by White Feet and Blackie," continued Mother Reindeer, "consisted of the tent skins and poles, sleeping skins, clothing, cooking pots, and part of the stock of dried fish. It was a big load, but it looked bigger than it really was. The other native people were very much surprised to see such a load drawn by two pastured caribou fawns.

"On the following day White Feet and Blackie were so tired and stiff that Dainten tethered them out in a good moss patch near the winter camp. His brother and sister kept watch over them.

The five doe fawns stayed near White Feet and Blackie. The hunter made them a small corral of alders, so that his little herd would be well protected from wolves in the nighttime.

"This hunter was a wise man. He knew that when wild caribou had been chased for several days they became very thin and poor. He now found that moss was not so strengthening to the fawns as meat was to the dogs. He wished to keep the little herd until they were grown up; so he took good care of them and allowed them to rest well before he took them back to the summer camp for another big load. You see, my son, the fierce hunter was becoming a good herder. The taming of the fawns had also tamed him and his family. The pastured caribou fawns were now called reindeer."

"Did they never see any of the wild caribou again?" White Sox asked.

"No, not to speak to," Mother Reindeer said, "but they soon became used to the ways of their human friends and were quite content. Before the November moon was gone, all the seal oil, dried fish, and meat had been hauled from the spit to the winter camp. The hunter had more than enough food stored up for his family; so he gave his attention to studying the ways and habits of caribou and taking care of his first little herd of reindeer.

"On clear days, and on nights when the moon was shining, he had the children take turns at watching the herd while it grazed. He took the sharp claws of the big Oogarook seals and fastened them to the ends of pieces of alder, about as big as your hoof. These made fine rakes or moss scratchers. The children used these scratchers for digging moss, which they put inside the corral for the fawns to eat on stormy days and dark nights. The first herder was a thoughtful man; he didn't want his herd to grow thin and poor."

"He was more thoughtful than some of our herders that Uncle Slim tells about," said White Sox.

Mother Reindeer nodded her head. "The first herder and his family had become so fond of their reindeer that they all seemed like one family," she said. "The human beings couldn't understand the caribou language, but White Feet and his band soon came to understand many native words. Dainten's brother was named Tahne-na. His sister's name was Tah-nes-ka."

White Sox had listened carefully to every word his mother had said. To him it was a very wonderful story. The more he thought about it, the more he wished to be like White Feet in mind as well as in body. After pondering for a while in silence, he said:

"I can see all the pictures now, mother — the careless caribou herd, the sneaking wolves, and the little band of fawns on the hill. Always the weakest of the herd were sacrificed in order that the stronger ones might escape and live a little

"'Our herders watch us at night only during the season when the ground is bare and we are inclined to scatter.'"

while longer. Always danger, unrest, and fear! I see the other pictures — one brave caribou fawn thinking and planning for the safety of those who depended on him, and boldly doing things no other caribou had ever dared to do. I see that first corral on the narrow spit, the first little sled and harness, the first little caribou serving man for the love of him. Each needed something the other had to give. The fawns needed protection. The human beings needed beasts of burden that would be a source of food, instead of those for whom food had to be provided."

White Sox had learned his lesson. Mother Reindeer felt proud of him.

"But listen, son," she said. "I have not yet finished my story. The first little herd of reindeer increased in numbers as the years went by, doubling their number every third spring. The two boys grew to manhood and married, and had families of their own. The old hunter and his wife died. There came a time when the herd was too large for the corrals. Dainten and Tah-ne-na had to take on new herders to help with the work. They now herded their reindeer in the open, day and night."

"We are not herded at night, mother," White Sox said.

"That is true, my son," said Mother Reindeer. "On this side of the big waters there are not so many wolves. Our herders watch us at night only during the season when the ground is bare and we are inclined to scatter."

"How did you get across the big waters, mother?"

"That is what I'm going to tell you now," she said.

"'My mother was a beautiful spotted reindeer.'"

XI

How Mother Reindeer Came to Alaska

"At last the herd became so big that it had to be divided," said Mother Reindeer. "Dainten had always claimed White Feet. Tah-ne-na had claimed Blackie. Now Dainten took all the spotted and white reindeer and moved toward the rising sun, where his wife's people lived. Tah-ne-na had only the dark reindeer for his herd. He moved toward the setting sun, where his wife's people had come from. They moved the two herds so far apart that they could never mingle again. Tah-ne-na's herd multiplied and stocked the shores toward the setting sun. Dainten's herd increased rapidly and spread along the shores toward the rising sun."

65

"You belonged to Dainten, didn't you, mother?" White Sox asked.

"Dainten and White Feet had been dead for ages and ages before I was born," said Mother Reindeer. "I belonged to one of the herds that descended from White Feet. My mother was a beautiful spotted reindeer, and my father was a great leader of a band of wild caribou. When I was a fawn, all the members of our family were roped and hobbled. We were taken on board a big floating corral and brought across the waters to a place some thirty days' journey from here. That floating corral was a long, narrow, smoky, noisy, quivering thing that moved over the surface of the waters toward the rising sun. It was a dreadful journey. Our mothers were too much scared to eat. The fawns were bleating all the time. For two suns there was no land anywhere in sight — nothing but water and fog, water and fog. We didn't know what the herders were going to do to us. We were all very much afraid.

"At last we came to another shore. The floating corral moved close up to the land and we were taken off. The place was strange. The people were strange. We were still very much afraid, but it was better to be on shore than on the floating corral. After a few days the floating corral came again and landed more reindeer. We were very glad to see our old friends, and we grew more contented.

"But in this new land we had strange men for

"'We were taken on board a big floating corral and brought
across the waters.'"

herders, to help our own herders who came with
us on the floating corral. They were too old to
learn how to take care of us. After a while we
had more new herders, men who wore shoes that
curved up at the toes, like boat sleds. They wore
high caps stuffed with feathers and spoke a strange
language. They threw the lasso straight, without
warning, instead of curling it three times around
overhead before shooting it out. But at last we
had some young men for herders, and they did
much better by us. Young people are like fawns;
they learn quickly. It was then that we began
to love the new land and our new herders."

"You've seen a great deal, mother, but how did
you get up here, thirty days' journey from the

place where you first lived in this new land?"
White Sox asked.

"That's another story, my son," Mother Reindeer said. "I will tell you about it after all your other lessons are learned. This much I will tell you now. One day some strange men came to our new land and talked with our herders. In a little while two reindeer herds on this side of the big waters were put together and driven north. The little bit of winter daylight had just begun to grow longer as we started. We didn't know where we were going, but we thought it must be on a long trip, because some sleds were loaded with food for the herders who were driving us.

"Our journey was on both land and sea. The sea was frozen over. We were on it two days and nights. Our sleds could not haul enough moss to feed the entire herd. The weak reindeer dropped on the ice and were left behind. Some ate too much of the salty frost that covered the ice. It made them thirsty. They became faint and were left behind. After we left the ice, our way lay across a mountainous country. When we had crossed that, wolves scented us and followed us many nights. It was a hard journey, much too hard and long for mothers at that time of the season.

"But at the end of the second moon we reached the place near the sea beach, where we now live. There we found many floating corrals among the ice and many strange men in houses. Then came the most terrible part of it all. Half the herd was butchered and hauled into the village where the men were."

"Mother!" exclaimed White Sox, in horror. "Did they kill all the males at once?"

"There were but few males in the herd," she answered. "Many of those killed were mothers and sisters. We didn't understand it. But your grandmother — her name was Spot — talked with a wild caribou that came near the herd. He told her that hunters had killed a great many wild caribou that winter and taken their bodies to the village. Together they reasoned it out that the men had no other kind of food, and that we had been brought there to keep that great herd of men from starving. Spot was a sled deer — "

"I thought you said she was my grandmother," White Sox broke in. "Did the reindeer mothers have to draw sleds after the big killing?"

"Spot did," said Mother Reindeer. "Your Uncle Slim was a fawn then. He trotted along beside her when she pulled the loaded sled. The herders made a little harness for him and worked him with his mother."

That was the end of Mother Reindeer's story. If you want to know more about the big killing at Point Barrow, you must read about how the whaling vessels were frozen in the ice there and how more than two hundred white men were reported starving during the coldest part of the long winter.

The herders sacrificed their reindeer to save the lives of these men. Of course Mother Reindeer did not know anything about whaling vessels; she called a ship a floating corral. But she was a wise old mother reindeer, for all that. Don't you think so?

"Away he dashed, with Mother Reindeer at his heels."

XII

White Sox Learns His Last Lesson

White Sox and his mother had been silent for a long time. But White Sox was not asleep; he had a great deal to think about, and he had just made up his mind that he must not be a baby any longer. He had been to school and had learned many lessons. He must be a leader now. And now was the time for him to make a start.

"Mother," he said, after he had looked about him this way and that, this way and that, "the moon is going to bed. I see a little streak of daylight creeping over the edge of the world. Let us take a run through that little valley below and

71

finish our lesson on the top of that ridge to the north of here, after we have eaten some breakfast."

"All right," said Mother Reindeer. She rose and stretched herself, but she did not offer any advice. She wanted to see what kind of leader White Sox would make.

First he tried to find which way the breeze was blowing. Then he turned his nose in that direction and sniffed several times. But not a thing could he scent. He looked very carefully everywhere. But not a thing could he see.

"Come on!" he cried; and down the knoll he started at a swift trot. He was thinking how much he wished to be like White Feet, but all the same he kept a sharp lookout to the east and to the west while he kept his nose turned to the north.

There was plenty of fine moss being trampled under his feet, but he did not stop to taste it. Up, up he went, to the very top of the next low ridge. When he saw that all was safe, he began to feed on the splendid moss under the blanket of snow.

Presently he looked up and said, "White Feet died a natural death, didn't he, mother?"

"Yes, so we are told," Mother Reindeer answered. "But he reached a ripe old age before he died."

White Sox ate awhile in silence; then he spoke again. "I think I understand it all now, mother.

"'In olden times the poor mothers were sacrificed to feed the
wolves.'"

White Feet was allowed to live because his services to man were of more value than his flesh
and skin. He was a great leader and a wise
teacher. He taught his herd and their off-
spring obedience to man and thankfulness for protection. He changed the order of things entirely.

"In olden times the poor mothers were sacrificed
to feed the wolves. Now the sons are sacrificed
to feed man, their protector. The sons pay the
debt which enables the mothers to live in peace
and safety."

"Yes, my son," said the proud mother, "and
you must know that the wild caribou have de-
creased in numbers year by year; but the rein-

deer, under the protection of man, have multiplied until now they form many mighty herds."

"That proves that the new way is better, mother," said White Sox. "Service and sacrifice for the males! That is now our law. That is why you didn't complain when my two big brothers were butchered."

Mother Reindeer nodded her head.

"Our worst enemies did us a kind turn when they stampeded White Feet and his little band into the hunter's tent," continued White Sox. "And man, our next worst enemy, did us a better turn when he taught us to serve him. Mother, if I am to live to a ripe old age and die a natural death, I must make myself so useful to man that my services will be of greater value than my flesh and skin. Isn't that right, mother?"

"That's the whole lesson, my son," Mother Reindeer said. "And now I will tell you that I have always wanted to be the mother of a second White Feet. I was pleased because you were marked like the great leader, but I am more pleased that you are able to think like him. A leader has to face many trials of courage and many temptations, and has great cares and responsibilities. It is only by overcoming all temptations and weaknesses and by boldly doing your duty that you become of great service to man and to your kind."

White Sox nodded his head. "Yes, mother," he said thoughtfully. "I've been worrying about my spoiled stockings and what the herd would think of these black ones, but now I'm glad my legs are black. By the time the hair comes next summer, and my new white stockings appear, I shall have learned many more lessons. I've one more question to ask. Do you ever wish to return to the land where White Feet lived?"

"No," said the kind old mother, "this is a better land for reindeer. The moss here is better. We have more timber, better sleds and harness, good herding dogs to help keep off our enemies, and good herders. I'm getting old, my son, but I hope to live to see you leader of the big herd — as wise and useful as your great ancestor."

"Thank you, mother dear," he said gently. "Thank you for telling me the big story. My! what a foolish fawn I was — wanting to stay with our wild cousins! How glad I am the wolves chased us away!"

He looked to the north, then to the west. He sniffed the air and turned this way and that, this way and that. At last he turned to the north and looked very steadily.

What do you think he saw?

A cloud of fog was rising from the ground. It was only a few miles ahead of them. The morning sky was bright and clear. The air was very cold.

"It looks like fog, but it can't be fog," he said doubtfully. Then he became excited.

"Mother, our big herd is right yonder where that fog bank is," he shouted.

"Yes, my son," said Mother Reindeer. "That fog cloud is their frozen breath."

"Come on!" cried White Sox.

Away he dashed, with Mother Reindeer at his heels.

Children of Grizzly

By Sadye M. Hageman
Formerly Teacher, Indian Public School
Colusa, California
in collaboration with
Alfred Oswald Shedd

WHO are the children of Grizzly? There is an Indian legend that the Indians are the children of Grizzly. So this book tells of the experiences of an Indian boy and girl who attended a modern Indian school. It includes information about Indian customs and Indian life which will appeal to children, and at the same time it points out ways of living which contribute to bodily strength and health.

There is in this book also, a plan for organizing the Grizzly Bear Tribe, a children's club based upon old-time Indian customs. Members of the Grizzly Bear Tribe learn to do many of the things told about in the book and work for honors in the practice of health.

There are more than entertaining stories and pictures in this book to arouse interest in the study of health. There are questions, things to do, things to think about, and things to be discussed in class. All of this is planned to give practical and readily useful information about health to children in elementary grades and to show them how to put health teachings into practice.

Cloth. x+176 pages. Illustrated. Price $1.00

WORLD BOOK COMPANY
Yonkers-on-Hudson, New York
2126 Prairie Avenue, Chicago

CPSIA information can be obtained
at www.ICGtesting.com
Printed in the USA
LVHW08*1041080718
583075LV00014B/327/P